M000074352

MONEY & WORK

10 STUDIES FOR INDIVIDUALS OR GROUPS

Carolyn Nystrom

With Notes for Leaders

IVP Connect

An imprint of InterVarsity Press
Downers Grove, Illinois

InterVarsity Press
P.O. Box 1400, Downers Grove, IL 60515-1426
World Wide Web: www.ivpress.com
E-mail: email@ivpress.com

©2011 by Carolyn Nystrom

InterVarsity Press® is the book-publishing division of InterVarsity Christian Fellowship/USA®, a movement of students and faculty active on campus at hundreds of universities, colleges and schools of nursing in the United States of America, and a member movement of the International Fellowship of Evangelical Students. For information about local and regional activities, write Public Relations Dept., InterVarsity Christian Fellowship/USA, 6400 Schroeder Rd., P.O. Box 7895, Madison, WI 53707-7895, or visit the IVCF website at <www.intervarsity.org>.

LifeGuide® is a registered trademark of InterVarsity Christian Fellowship.

All Scripture quotations, unless otherwise indicated, are taken from the Holy Bible, New International Version®. NIV®. Copyright ©1973, 1978, 1984 by International Bible Society. Used by permission of Zondervan Publishing House. All rights reserved.

Parts of this guide were originally published in Living in the World by Carolyn Nystrom (Downers Grove, Ill.: InterVarsity Press, 1992), ©1992 by Carolyn Nystrom.

Cover image: Dennis Flaherty

ISBN 978-0-8308-3142-5

Printed in the United States of America ∞

g green press INITIATIVE *InterVarsity Press is committed to protecting the environment and to the responsible use of natural resources. As a member of Green Press Initiative we use recycled paper whenever possible. To learn more about the Green Press Initiative, visit <www.greenpressinitiative.org>.*

P	18	17	16	15	14	13	12	11	10	9	8	7	6	5	4	3	2	1
Y	26	25	24	23	22	21	20	19	18	17	16	15	14	13	12	11

Contents

Getting the Most Out of *Money and Work*

Work and money used to be fairly uncomplicated topics in my mind. I was one of those students who worked her way through college—with the help of a scholarship that paid about one quarter of my expenses. My formula for balancing work and money was fairly simple: work long enough, hard enough, so that I didn't have to worry about either one.

Unfortunately, I did not always calculate sleep and study time into the equation. For example, one semester I scheduled an all-nighter for myself each week because I worked a late shift one day and an early shift the next, so why bother to go to bed? I figured I might as well use what little night was left to study. I think that was the year that my grades and my weight dropped dangerously low—and it was the beginning of my growing awareness that having money and work in themselves does not necessarily mean that all is well with life.

A few decades, many added responsibilities and a shifting world economy have caused me to see that my college-era formula, while getting me through school, did not come near addressing the complex relationship between money and work, nor did it look at the undercurrent of power and time that influences both subjects.

In 2008, people of all ages were forced to take a particularly hard look at the subject of work and money. It was a time when former bankers were bagging groceries, when 401ks saved for retirement withered overnight, when fresh college graduates moved back home because they couldn't get a job, when whole cities like Detroit hit the rust bin. Cash for Gold shops sprouted in formerly wealthy suburbs—as did clothing resale shops. Larger big-box stores closed their doors and emptied their merchandise, leaving once thriving malls looking strangely withered. Newspaper listings of home foreclosures grew pages long.

Months later as the world economy began once again to creep upward, people continued to look cautiously over their shoulders at work and money. Would the upturn continue or was this just a temporary pause in a long-term downward spiral? Was it safe now to set a retirement date? Should the college graduate get his own place even though he might need temporary help with the rent? How much lower than money spent should a homeowner now drop her selling price? Was it safe yet to resign from an unbearable job?

The Bible is not a textbook on economics, but it does offer much personal guidance on how to navigate both riches and poverty, employment and beggary. As we might expect, principles, values, motives and faith rank far higher in these biblical accounts than any formula for financial success. Above all we encounter the character of Almighty God, who "gives us richly all things to enjoy" and expects us to be equally generous in his name. So we study God's value system through his own written words. We look twice at the ancient book of wisdom, Ecclesiastes. Four times we look at the direct teachings of Jesus. Once we emulate the prayers of the great King David. Twice we read from a letter by the apostle Paul, looking over the shoulder of the original recipients. And finally we look at what is perhaps the most ancient of biblical books, Job. These texts of holy Scripture will take us much farther toward wisdom than did my simple college-era dictum. May we enjoy God's gifts of work and money, veer away from misuse of their parallel gifts of time and power, and do it all with diligence, kindness, generosity and great thanks—for his glory.

Suggestions for Individual Study

1. As you begin each study, pray that God will speak to you through his Word.

2. Read the introduction to the study and respond to the personal reflection question or exercise. This is designed to help you focus on God and on the theme of the study.

3. Each study deals with a particular passage so that you can delve into the author's meaning in that context. Read and reread the passage to be studied. The questions are written using the language of the New International Version, so you may wish to use that version of the Bible. The New Revised Standard Version is also recommended.

4. This is an inductive Bible study, designed to help you discover for yourself what Scripture is saying. The study includes three types of questions. *Observation* questions ask about the basic facts: who, what, when, where and how. *Interpretation* questions delve into the meaning of the passage. *Application* questions help you discover the implications of the text for growing in Christ. These three keys unlock the treasures of Scripture.

Write your answers to the questions in the spaces provided or in a personal journal. Writing can bring clarity and deeper understanding of yourself and of God's Word.

5. It might be good to have a Bible dictionary handy. Use it to look up any unfamiliar words, names or places.

6. Use the prayer suggestion to guide you in thanking God for what you have learned and to pray about the applications that have come to mind.

7. You may want to go on to the suggestion under "Now or Later," or you may want to use that idea for your next study.

Suggestions for Members of a Group Study

1. Come to the study prepared. Follow the suggestions for individual study mentioned above. You will find that careful preparation will greatly enrich your time spent in group discussion.

2. Be willing to participate in the discussion. The leader of your group will not be lecturing. Instead, he or she will be encouraging the members of the group to discuss what they have learned. The leader will be asking the questions that are found in this guide.

3. Stick to the topic being discussed. Your answers should be based on the verses which are the focus of the discussion and not on outside authorities such as commentaries or speakers. These studies focus on a particular passage of Scripture. Only rarely should you refer to other portions of the Bible. This allows for everyone to participate in in-depth study on equal ground.

4. Be sensitive to the other members of the group. Listen attentively when they describe what they have learned. You may be surprised by their insights! Each question assumes a variety of answers.

Many questions do not have "right" answers, particularly questions that aim at meaning or application. Instead the questions push us to explore the passage more thoroughly.

When possible, link what you say to the comments of others. Also, be affirming whenever you can. This will encourage some of the more hesitant members of the group to participate.

5. Be careful not to dominate the discussion. We are sometimes so eager to express our thoughts that we leave too little opportunity for others to respond. By all means participate! But allow others to also.

6. Expect God to teach you through the passage being discussed and through the other members of the group. Pray that you will have an enjoyable and profitable time together, but also that as a result of the study you will find ways that you can take action individually and/or as a group.

7. Remember that anything said in the group is considered confidential and should not be discussed outside the group unless specific permission is given to do so.

8. If you are the group leader, you will find additional suggestions at the back of the guide.

1
What Is
My Time Worth?

Joseph stood up from a battered basement chair, stretched his shoulders that now seemed permanently crunched into computer slump and said, "I think it's working okay now."

"I don't know how to thank you," said his neighbor Neil—a good two decades Joseph's senior—with a grin. "It must be nice having been born with a computer chip. I don't think I'll ever understand these things." He gestured toward his relic Dell. "Let me take you out to breakfast some time next week. Making her sing again has got to be worth a platter of bacon and eggs."

"Yeah, sure," Joseph said, glancing at his watch: 9 p.m. He'd left for the office at dawn and hadn't yet had dinner. Being the neighborhood techy had its drawbacks.

GROUP DISCUSSION. Are you more likely to be generous or protective with your time? How and why?

PERSONAL REFLECTION. When you think of your own time well spent or your own time badly spent, what images come to mind? Talk to God about these.

Two poems from Ecclesiastes—one near the beginning of the book and one at the end—offer some much-needed perspective on time. *Read Ecclesiastes 3:1-14.*

1. What do you appreciate about this poem?

2. Scan the fourteen sets of couplets in 3:1-8. Which of these twenty-eight kinds of time seems most descriptive of your life right now (e.g., planting, weeping, mending, being silent, etc.)? How?

3. What burden does the author describe in verses 9-11?

4. What does it mean that God has "set eternity in the human heart"? When have you sensed this deposit from God in yourself?

5. Look ahead to your plans for next Thursday. How can you begin now to anticipate that day with its content as a gift from God?

6. Turn to the end of Ecclesiastes and read 12:1-8 aloud. Why do you think the author begins this poem with the command to "remember"?

7. What pictures of the aging process do you see in verses 1-8?

8. Now read aloud Ecclesiastes 12:9-14, an epilogue to all that has been previously written. What wisdom do you find here for how we should view and use our time?

9. "'Meaningless! Meaningless!' says the Teacher. 'Everything is meaningless!'" (12:8). The word *meaningless* appears more than forty times in the book of Ecclesiastes. As you reflect on time's worth as it has been revealed throughout chapters 3 and 12, how would you respond to the Teacher's complaint?

10. In view of time's value as reflected in these texts, including the final verses of the book, how would you advise Joseph to respond the next time his neighbor calls him about another computer glitch?

11. Consider again the description of your current life setting that you selected in response to question two. How might you need to adjust the way you're using your time in this season of your life?

"[God] has made everything beautiful in its time. He has also set eternity in the hearts of men. . . . I know that everything God does will endure forever; nothing can be added to it and nothing taken from it. God does it so that men will revere him" (Ecclesiastes 3:11, 14). God always was, is and will be eternal. We mortals are stuck in time for now—which is itself a gift. In prayer express your reverence to God.

Now or Later

"I know that there is nothing better for men than to be happy and do good while they live. That everyone may eat and drink, and find satisfaction in all his toil—this is the gift of God" (Ecclesiastes 3:12-13).

For three days keep an hour-by-hour time log. Note even those unexpected interruptions—and how you dealt with them. At the end of your three-day experiment, reread Ecclesiastes 3:9-14. In view of your growing understanding of that text, give yourself a "satisfaction rating" for each half-day segment. Bear in mind that our best use of time points toward eternity—even though we are not yet there.

2

Use or Lose?

Rosa has wanted to be a doctor as long as she can remember. She thinks maybe it started at age six when she stood in line for her first visit with a doctor—a school check-up from the gentle gray-haired lady with a blue coat and a stethoscope. She worked hard in high school, kept her grades above average, worked an after-school job to save money and graduated—the first of her immigrant family to do so.

At college she signed up for premed classes but quickly floundered. Chemistry kept her up all night with little gain in understanding, and whole sections of calculus might as well have been written in Chinese. After two years of near failure she switched to nursing, and graduated on schedule. Meanwhile her friends from her premed days trooped off to medical school. Now Rosa is job-hunting, ready to carry out *their* orders as doctors.

But does she still want to work in medicine? As a nurse?

GROUP DISCUSSION. What are some of Rosa's career options at this point? What might she be thinking and feeling about each of them?

PERSONAL REFLECTION. What are some areas of your life where you feel cheated of opportunity—and how do you handle it?

The parable of the talents is the middle story of three parables Jesus told his disciples to help them prepare for his return. *Read Matthew 25:14-30.*

1. Suppose you are sitting among the disciples listening to Jesus tell this story. What do you want to ask him?

2. What do the master's words and actions in verses 14-23 reveal about his character?

3. Three times Jesus uses the word *entrusted* (vv. 14, 20, 22). What does this word communicate about the relationship between the master and his servants?

4. Why do you think the master doesn't give an equal amount to each of the three servants?

5. What has God entrusted to you?

6. Focus on verses 24-30. If the servant is as frightened of his master as he claims, why do you think he didn't deposit the money with the bankers?

7. What had this servant failed to understand about his master?

8. Who does not trust whom in this story?

With what results?

9. The master speaks of his third servant as "worthless" (v. 30). What all does this imply?

10. Select a talent that God has entrusted to you, perhaps the one you named for question five. How might you use that talent in a way that prepares for the kind of reunion with Jesus experienced by the master's first two servants?

11. Suppose you are having lunch with Rosa just as she begins her job search. Without mentioning this parable but drawing on its implications, what might you say to her?

Pray, thanking God for something or someone he has "entrusted" to you. Begin now to seek his direction on how you can invest that asset in a way that might cause him to say to you, "Well done, good and faithful servant! Come and share your master's happiness!"

Now or Later

Make a list of the jobs you've had, from your very first one to your current or most recent one. Next to each listing, note something that you learned about yourself and something you learned about God during each job.

Consider how you might draw on this experience as you continue with whatever work, whether paid or unpaid, occupies most of your time in this era of your life. Write out any thoughts that come to mind.

3

Why Work?

Conroy's friend Zane doesn't work. Actually he does work sometimes, but not often and not well. That was okay when Zane was single. He would work for a while and save a few dollars, and then quit his job, take a road trip, enjoy the savings, come back to his rented room and unpaid bills, find another job, pay off some of his bills, and hit the road again.

But now Zane is married and has a small child. Road trips aren't much of an option these days, but his work patterns have not improved. He works a while, then gets mad at the boss and quits. Or some days he just sleeps late and doesn't go in—and gets fired. At other times he's at work but can't seem to measure up to job expectations.

Last night Zane drove his fifteen-year-old pickup to Conroy's house and, while scuffing a spot on the lawn with his worn sneaker and with his eyes to the ground, asked for a loan. His landlord is threatening eviction, his wife hasn't been to the grocery store for two weeks, and the baby needs medication. He has no current job.

Conroy and Zane are both Christians, although they belong to different churches. What should Conroy do?

GROUP DISCUSSION. Put yourself for a moment inside Zane's skin. What do you think he feels? What are his fears? his hopes? How do you think he explains his work patterns to himself?

PERSONAL REFLECTION. Do you tend to over- or undervalue work?

How does this impact the way you think of the "Zanes" in your life? Stop right now and pray for one of them.

The Thessalonian Christians were also wrestling with issues related to work. Near the end of Paul's second letter to them, he provides some guidelines. *Read 2 Thessalonians 3:6-15.*

1. What all do you see here that shows Paul's value of work?

2. Paul had already warned this particular church about work problems, and he had written in a similar vein to the church of Ephesus and its pastor, Timothy. Read 1 Thessalonians 4:11-12, Ephesians 4:28 and 1 Timothy 5:8. Using these texts as well as 2 Thessalonians 3:6-15, create as many as a dozen sentences, each beginning with the words, "I should work because . . ."

3. Zane is still a young man in his twenties. In view of the warnings in the texts above, what can you see of his future if he continues his current path?

4. What types of work have you done in your life?

Take another look at the list of reasons to work that you compiled in response to question two. How have your past jobs and roles fulfilled some of those purposes?

5. As you think through the four texts above, is choosing to work or not work (whether in a paid or unpaid position) a matter of individual preference for Christians? Why or why not?

6. Most Christians, even those who work hard, encounter tempting "time wasters." When you are tempted to not work at some current responsibility, what distraction are you likely to give in to?

Review again the list you made in question two. If you overindulge in this favorite distraction, what harm might come to you or others? What good might you miss?

7. What do you think is the difference between idleness and leisure?

8. In spite of Paul's various warnings about idleness, he closes his second letter to the Thessalonians with, "Do not regard him as an enemy, but warn him as a brother" (2 Thessalonians 3:15). Immediately after Zane's request for a loan, how might Conroy begin to treat Zane as a brother?

9. How can you reflect the character of Paul (and, ultimately, Jesus) as you work?

as you respond to someone like Zane?

Examine your thoughts and feelings about people who do not work or do not work hard enough. Ask God to reveal to you any pride or unwarranted self-protection and confess these shortcomings to him.

Now or Later

Review all four texts about work and review the values implied in each: 2 Thessalonians 3:6-15; Ephesians 4:28; 1 Thessalonians 4:11-12; 1 Timothy 5:8. What options does this passage suggest for Conroy? What do you think about those different options?

Create a game plan for Conroy that involves his church and Zane's church so that Zane can grow in these values, if he is willing, and make steps toward self-sufficiency, including responsible care for his family. If there is a real "Zane" in your life, pair up with another person or group to help you think through and work out these plans. How do you think your response, and churches' responses, to people like Zane could affect nonbelievers?

4

Trustworthy?

Buck is getting laid off. For three years he has managed an accounts receivable department for an electronics distribution center. He likes his boss, likes his office, likes his working conditions—and he does good work. But a corporate buyout is taking his whole department to Atlanta, and Buck is not among the few chosen to move with the company. Even the building will be sold. In a month, he'll be jobless.

What should he do in this month? Work hard at getting the books up to date? Collect as many accounts as possible? Or should he slow down collections, give the creditors a few weeks of grace during the transition? Should he call in "sick" to use up his accumulated sick leave? Take home a few warehouse items before they get shipped south or tossed in the trash bin?

Could he get a job with one of the creditor companies? Would they look at him more favorably if the bills weren't so prompt this month? Or if a bill or two got "lost"?

GROUP DISCUSSION. Have you ever lost a job? Describe what happened and how you felt.

PERSONAL REFLECTION. Explore your inner compass of honesty. How would you answer some of Buck's questions if you were absolutely certain that no one would ever know?

This text is one of the most confusing of Jesus' parables, perhaps deliberately so, because he had two sets of listeners: his disciples and the Pharisees who "loved money." So Jesus has them look at two kinds of future (the immediate physical future and the eternal future) and the value system that supports each. *Read Luke 16:1-15.*

1. What do you think of the people in this parable?

2. What problems does each character in this story face?

3. From the details given in the entire text, what do you know of the manager's motives?

4. Jesus concludes the parable by noting that, even though the owner knew his manager was cheating him (or at least not managing his finances well), he commends him for being shrewd. Do you agree that the manager was shrewd? Why or why not?

5. In verse 9, Jesus begins his explanation of the parable by saying, "I tell you, use worldly wealth . . ." Of course, we can't buy our way into heaven, which the whole New Testament insists. But how could you invest your time or money in a way that would gain friends who would welcome you into "eternal dwellings"?

6. How is this eternal life-view different from the shrewd manager's?

7. What practical principles for managing someone else's property do you find in verses 9-15?

8. How might you use some of these principles if you were interviewing Buck for his next job?

9. Consider what you know of good business practice and Jesus' teachings for those he calls "people of the light." What similarities and what differences do you find?

10. Jesus proclaims, "You cannot serve both God and Money" (v. 13). In what situations in your own life do you find yourself having to choose between the two?

11. What have you seen happen, either in your life or in the lives of others, when money is chosen over God, and vice versa?

Ask God to reveal to you ways that you can invest both your time and your money in eternity.

Now or Later

For one month keep a detailed record of all money that you receive and all money that you spend. At the end of that time, group expenses together into various categories: food, housing, recreation, transportation, utilities, etc. When you're finished, study the patterns you see in how you acquired and used money in the past month. Make notes to yourself about how well you've managed the money God has allowed you and where you might improve next month in either spending or income.

At the close of this budget analysis, estimate how much money you spent toward things that might be broadly defined as "eternal."

5

What's Tempting About Power?

Marcos gets it done. It's been that way as long as he can remember, whether he was designing and building LEGO towers at age eight, mowing the lawns of ten neighbors at age fourteen or reading *all* of *A Tale of Two Cities* for his junior literature class. Now an international executive in intelligence technology, he can attend a virtual meeting by international phone while texting his wife a reminder about their son's basketball practice from the back seat of a cab on the way to the airport in Madrid—and do it all with a smile if necessary. When he hires workers he does so by the dozen to fill up a task team in Chicago, perhaps, or maybe Beijing. Firings, which he always regrets, are done with much the same efficiency.

Marcos knows the temptations of power; he battles them every day. He also knows power's responsibilities—along with some of its privileges.

GROUP DISCUSSION. What is one area where you would like to have more power than you do? Why?

PERSONAL REFLECTION. How would you answer the title question, "What's tempting about power?"

Jesus had much to say about the use and abuse of power. These three scenes from near the end of his life offer some poignant truths about the way his followers are to view and use the power they've been given. *Read Matthew 20:1-28.*

___

1. Find as many examples of the use of power as you can in these three scenes.

___

2. Focus on the parable that Jesus tells in verses 1-16. As you visualize this parable, which scene is most compelling to you? Why?

___

3. Why do you think the landowner continues hiring fieldworkers all day?

___

4. Study verses 13-15. What does this suggest about the landowner's motive for the way he uses his power?

___

5. Notice the way Jesus opens and closes his story (vv. 1-2 and 16). Through this parable, what might the disciples begin to know about their place in the kingdom of heaven?

6. Focus on verses 17-19. In view of this scene, would you say that power is good? evil? something else?

7. In verses 20-27, what are the different intentions of the various characters with regard to power?

8. Reread Jesus' summary of his teachings about power in verses 25-28. Marcos is a capable corporate executive; he is also a devout Christian. If you were his pastor or accountability partner, what symptoms would you suggest he watch for as he guards himself against loving his power too much—or misusing the power that God has given him?

What are some specific ways that Marcos could live out the principles Jesus teaches in verses 24-28?

9. What is one setting where you know you tend to "lord it over" other people as verse 25 describes?

What "inner housekeeping" could you begin that might move you more toward the servant style of leadership that Jesus asks of his followers?

10. Select a group context that is important to you—perhaps your church, a student group, your family or your workplace. When and how have you seen someone exercise power in the way that Jesus teaches us to do here?

Pray, thanking God for the servant leaders who have graced your life.

Now or Later

Work and money, time and power. All four of these ingredients mingle in the text studied above. While *Money and Work* is the title of this study guide, it might also have been appropriately titled *Time and Power.* Sin in the areas of money or work often connects to a misuse of time and/or power. But if we are able to move our time and our power into the God-inspired perspective of serving others, both work and money can become assets instead of liabilities. Instead of falling under their temptations, we might actually develop the twin virtues of *generosity* and *humility.*

For one week try to be particularly alert whenever the course of your day puts you in touch with either work or money. In each situation look for an opportunity to serve with *generosity* or *humility.*

6

How Much Is Enough?

Howard and Martha bend over the kitchen table with bank statements, checkbooks, a calculator, a long-range calendar and stacks of paper scattered all directions. In this fortieth year of their marriage, long-range financial planning has taken a new dimension. The kids are raised and mostly self-supporting. The house is paid off—except for that small equity loan. But one more financial milestone looms ahead: retirement. After decades of hard work they don't expect an extravagant lifestyle in retirement, but they also don't want to become a charity case for their children.

How much longer should they work? How much income will social security and retirement benefits pay—at what year? How much savings must they accumulate? Should they invest in updating their house or put any extra money into savings? Or should they invest instead in experience—maybe that longed-for trip to Africa? Should they buy long-term care insurance? Or plan to enter a retirement community? How long will their current car hold out? What if one of them gets sick—too soon? Realistically, how much money is enough?

GROUP DISCUSSION. What circumstances say "enough" to you?

PERSONAL REFLECTION. What kind of financial planning do you need

to do in the near future? How might your value system regarding
work and money influence the way you plan?

The ancient writer of Ecclesiastes helps us explore the human concept of enough. *Read Ecclesiastes 5:8-20.*

1. What title would you give to each segment of this passage?

Verses 8-9:

Verses 10-17:

Verses 18-20:

2. Describe the financial system outlined in verses 8-9.

3. How might the people benefit if even one official in this chain follows Jesus' teaching about power? (See your work in study five.)

4. Look again at verses 10-17. Pick one sentence from this series of
sayings and describe an experience you've had or observed that illustrates that sentence.

5. Suppose that you came to believe as absolutely true the life-view of work and money of the people described in verses 10-17. What would you begin to do and say and become?

6. In verses 18-20, the writer of Ecclesiastes turns to God for the first time in this chapter. What gifts from God might workers receive, even though they must work hard for any money that comes to them?

7. How do your mind and body change when you set out to *enjoy* something?

8. Consider the task at hand for Howard and Martha. What decisions would they make if they emphasize the life-view of those described in verses 10-17?

How would they plan differently if they emphasize the life-view expressed in verses 18-20?

9. In a previous study we saw Jesus warn his disciples, "You cannot serve both God and Money" (Luke 16:13). How might the teachings of Ecclesiastes 5:18-20 help you to worship God while you're actually doing your work and earning your income?

10. Suppose you were able to sit down with a man who is eighty years old and has lived by this final paragraph for several decades. What would you expect him to talk about?

11. Ask yourself the question that titles this study: "How much is enough?" In view of this study from Ecclesiastes, how might you begin to answer that question?

Take time right now to thank God for a task you've done—and enjoyed—in the past twenty-four hours. Then commit to consciously enjoying at least one task each day this week. At the end of each day, thank God for that gift—both the task and the ability to enjoy it.

Now or Later

Focus on one long-range financial goal that you need to make at your particular life stage: Accumulating a down payment? Paying off a loan or a bill? Saving for college expenses? Living within your weekly income? Saving for a trip? Planning retirement? Something else?

In about one page, write out a plan that sets out action steps, checkpoints, dates, possible adjustments and a specific goal. Include several "what if" scenarios with potential solutions. Post your plan in an obvious place where you can check your progress at weekly or monthly intervals. Then begin one of your first steps toward that goal this week.

7

Does My Property Own Me?

Luke 12:13-34

Kelly was sick and tired of clutter—sick and tired, for example, of pawing through drawers, a closet and eventually the laundry hamper when all she needed was one pair of size-four kids pants for the third potty accident of the day. A full quarter-of-an-hour went by before she found what she needed and returned to the living room, now awash with toys but nobody playing. Three pairs of eyes were glued to Dora—or was that Spider-Man this time?—with Terry, the soggy three-year-old, sucking a sticky thumb. How had he gotten into the marshmallows?

It was at that moment that Kelly took a silent oath: *I'm cleaning out! Every closet, every drawer, every cupboard, stripped to the walls, with everything in them sorted and then sold or donated. Any remaining necessities can be kept—but only if in constant current use.* She'd start with her own closet.

Two nights later and hours after bedtime, Kelly stands in a circle of clothes, her empty closet (now thoroughly washed) behind her. How has she ever managed to accumulate forty-three T-shirts? Trouble is, she really, really likes at least thirty-five of them.

GROUP DISCUSSION. When do you wonder if you might have too much—or too little?

PERSONAL REFLECTION. Imagine that Jesus said directly to you, "Watch out! Be on your guard against all kinds of greed." What specifically do you think he might be talking about?

In this section of Luke's Gospel, Jesus tells a story about crops and barns and then illustrates that story in response to a question. *Read Luke 12:13-34.*

1. How might you have answered the request presented to Jesus in verse 13?

2. Examine the story in verses 16-21. What do you find worrisome in this parable?

3. Notice Jesus' summary of his story in verse 21. How might this farmer have done a more thorough job of future planning?

4. Jesus begins the next section with the words, "Do not worry . . ." How do his illustrations of lilies, ravens and flocks help with the kind of worry his parable introduces?

5. Review the entire text of Luke 12:13-34 and list each of Jesus' commands.

Select one, attach your name to it and repeat the command. What is one way, appropriate to your circumstances, that you could put that command into action?

---

6. Two times, in mini-summaries of his teaching, Jesus speaks of the heart (vv. 29-31 and again in v. 34). What are some ways that a Christ-follower might nurture the kind of heart Jesus seems to expect of his people?

---

7. "Watch out! Be on your guard against all kinds of greed; a man's life does not consist in the abundance of his possessions" (v. 15). This admonition is part of Jesus' response to the inquirer who felt robbed of his inheritance—but also to all others present—and serves as an introduction to the rest of what Jesus has to say about possessions. What might this admonition mean to a person who has few, if any, possessions?

What might it mean to a person who owns much?

8. What is spiritually dangerous about greed?

9. What does this section of Luke's Gospel reveal of God's character?

10. Assume that you are standing in the crowd when Jesus tells his story of the talents in Matthew 25:14-30 and again when he teaches the parable before us today. How could you put the two stories together and give Kelly some advice about her closet?

11. In view of all that you have gained from this text and from your own experience, what symptoms would cause you to suspect that property is beginning to own its owner?

Thank God for those possessions most dear to you, naming them one by one. Offer them and yourself to his service.

Now or Later

What could you not bear to lose or give away? Why? Examine your heart for any symptoms of greed and also for evidence of trust in God.

8

How Much Is Too Much?

1 Timothy 6:3-10, 17-20

Madabuku is a third-generation Christian living in Lagos, Nigeria, inland from Africa's northwest coast. A young man just finishing college with a degree in business, Madabuku is starting now with a financial plan: He will work almost around the clock for ten years while living in his parents' home. He will invest wisely. At age thirty he will begin to design and build a home. At age thirty-five he will find and marry a wife. Five years later they will begin a family of two children. And he will become rich.

Madabuku has seen African poverty, and he wants no part of it. He believes that poverty comes from laziness, poor planning and God's displeasure over sin. So he will live a clean life, pray every day, contribute generously to his church—and not anger Almighty God. He can already picture an aviary in his new home overlooking distant mountains, a gift from God who loves to reward his people.

GROUP DISCUSSION. Describe the point in your life when you were the poorest you've ever been.

PERSONAL REFLECTION. When and how have your current feelings about money come about?

Today's passage comes from the closing paragraphs of a letter of instruction that the apostle Paul wrote to his young friend Timothy, the pastor of a church in first-century Ephesus. *Read 1 Timothy 6:3-10 and 17-20.*

---

1. What advice do you find here that could be valuable to a young pastor of a newly formed church?

---

2. Look more carefully at verses 3-5. What kind of atmosphere would you expect to find in a church where people do not "agree to the sound instruction of our Lord Jesus Christ"?

---

3. Do a quick review of the passages from the four studies where you examined what Jesus taught about work and money. Try to state in one sentence Jesus' main teaching in each text.

Matthew 25:14-30:

Luke 16:1-15:

Matthew 20:1-18:

Luke 12:13-34:

4. What do you find spiritually dangerous about the idea of godliness being a means to financial gain (1 Timothy 6:5)?

5. Thoughtfully reread 1 Timothy 6:6-10. Suppose you were able to have a quiet personal conversation with Madabuku. What would you hope he might understand from this text?

6. Paul says in verse 10, "For the love of money is a root of all kinds of evil." What kinds of evil can grow out of an overconcern about money if a person is rich? if a person is poor?

7. In verse 6 Paul offers an alternative to the kind of striving described in the first paragraph. Here he says, "Godliness with contentment is great gain." When you picture a person who lives by this principle, what do you see?

8. Focus on verses 17-19, noticing the specific commands that Paul gives to people who are already rich. How might practicing these principles about money lead to the "great gain" of contentment?

9. Why do you think Paul does not command the rich to give all of their money away so that they become poor?

---

10. In his poem "Scots' Form in the Suburbs," historian Mark Noll describes needy Christians at the Communion table as "the poor and rich hemmed in alike by cash." What have you found in this study that might help you be less "hemmed in" by your own current financial situation?

In prayer, ask God to show you how you can prepare in the course of each day for the "coming age" and the "life that is truly life."

Now or Later

"Godliness with contentment is great gain." Place this statement in a spot that often catches your eye. Find various ways to keep it in your mind: memorize it, meditate on it, illustrate it, pray over it, try to acquire its values. At the end of a month, reread all of today's text and, in prayer, confess any sins that come to mind as well as celebrate the ways God has grown you in this area. Then ask for his continued help in the month ahead.

9

Why Give?

Ten-year-old Jason wriggled his way along the church pew—just six inches farther from his mom—and fished into his pockets. Right pocket: a couple of dimes and his collection of soda-can rings tied together with twine from his dad's toolbox. Only a slight jingle; his mom wouldn't notice. Left pocket: his dollar bill. Mom had made a special point of checking that he had that in his pocket before they left the house. He'd spent all afternoon Saturday helping Ned Spinks clean out his barn and had gotten ten dollars for his work. Mom seemed to think one of those ten dollars should go to the church.

Jason wasn't so sure. Nine dollars would go a long way toward that TRANSFORMERS game he was saving for, but ten dollars would go even further. It was his money; he'd earned it. Maybe he could slip a dime into the offering basket instead. The offertory music is starting. What to do?

GROUP DISCUSSION. How do you feel when you see a church offering basket coming your direction?

PERSONAL REFLECTION. When you give money to your church or some other Christian organization, what is most often your motive?

King David walks toward the end of his life. God will not permit him to build the temple, but David can prepare his people for that great event. *Read 1 Chronicles 29:1-20.*

1. Focus on verses 1-9 and picture yourself in this scene. Describe what you hear and see and feel.

2. Note each mention of God in verses 1-9. In view of David's challenge to them, what all might they understand of their relationship to God?

3. What might you realistically borrow from this scene for your own church or fellowship group?

4. Focus on David's prayer (vv. 10-20). In verses 10-13, David concentrates the first part of his prayer on praising God. What does he appreciate about God's character?

5. Select one of those qualities of God highlighted by David. Why do you appreciate that aspect of God's nature?

6. Prayerfully reread aloud David's prayer of praise in verses 10-13. After you read the words of verse 13, stop and pray, praising and thanking God in single sentences for who he is as you have experienced him and for what he has given you that you have enjoyed.

7. After David focuses on God, he turns the focus on himself and God's people (vv. 14-17). In what different areas does David illustrate their relationship to God?

8. How might these word pictures continue to affect the way the Israelites choose to use their wealth?

9. David ended his fundraising challenge with the words, "Now, who is willing to consecrate himself today to the LORD?" (v. 5). What all do you think that meant in their setting?

What all does it mean in your own setting?

10. Think back to the opening scene of this study. If you were Jason's mom or dad, how might you adapt David's prayer in verses 17-19 when you pray for the future of your son Jason?

Pray, beginning with David's words, "I know, my God, that you test the heart and are pleased with integrity." Then add whatever seems important to you as you speak from your current relationship with God.

Now or Later

David says in verse 14: "Everything comes from you." What all has God given you? In five minutes write down everything that comes to mind in answer to that question. Circle several items on your list and note ideas for using each of those gifts in ways that express thanks to God.

10

What If I Lose It All?

It is the evening of Thanksgiving Day, and Carol can't remember a more satisfying day. Four children and spouses, eight grandchildren—from highchair age to teenage stage—a table laden with crusty turkey stuffed with her own grandmother's dressing, salad, sides and pies brought by the kids (each showing off their best), a time of thoughtful conversation just before dessert with each person giving thanks to God for some special gift or event of the past year. Even little Melinda yelled "Cookies" from her highchair at just the right moment. Football in the living room, help in the kitchen, toys and games on the floor, then farewell hugs and kisses with promises of doing it again at Christmas, a mere month away.

Right now her husband, Harvey, is snoozing on the sofa, lulled to sleep by the hum of football commentary and the dishwasher, as Carol stands in grateful silence. And then, unbidden, a chilling thought: *What if I lost it all?*

GROUP DISCUSSION. "Why do bad things happen to good people?" This is a perennial question for people of faith. What answers have you heard to this question? Which do you find unsatisfying? Why?

PERSONAL REFLECTION. Do a little soul-digging about your own losses or feared losses. Which do you find the most troubling? Why?

Job is the story of an ancient man. It touches our fears—and our faith. *Read Job 1:1-22 and 19:17-27.*

---

1. What pictures form in your mind of Job and his setting as described in 1:1-5?

---

2. Examine the unseen conflict recorded in 1:6-12. What all do you find unsettling about this scene?

---

3. Beginning at verse 1:13, focus on Job as his day unfolds. What words or questions come to your mind as you try to absorb the impact of the events that occur?

---

4. If you were Job's friend, what would you likely do or say by the end of 1:22?

---

5. Compare the scene of 1:20-22 with the scene in 1:6-12. Who is on trial, and for what?

---

6. What all does worship mean for Job in this context (1:20)?

7. How might 1:22 serve as both a reassurance and a warning for us?

8. Read the scene in Job 19:17-27 that occurs many weeks later. Job's plight has not gotten better; in fact, it has gotten worse. Why might you both pity and admire Job at this point?

9. By faith Job speaks of a cosmic scene in 19:25-27. What does this scene reveal about the nature of God and the future of his people?

10. Meditate for a few minutes on Job's words in 19:26: "Yet in my flesh I will see God." What did this statement mean for Job?

What does it mean for you?

11. How might Job's experience and his faith statements influence how you manage your own losses or feared losses?

Pray aloud Job's faith statement of Job 19:25-27.

Now or Later

Page through hymnals or music scores to find various versions of Job's faith statement as it has been set to music. If these are not available to you, enjoy the words of this version written by Charles Wesley in 1742 and often sung to music adapted from the *Messiah*, which was composed by George Frederick Handel in 1741. Sing, meditate, illustrate or pray as is appropriate for your personal setting.

> *I know that my Redeemer lives, and ever prays for me;*
> *A token of his love he gives, a pledge of liberty.*
> *I find him lifting up my head; he brings salvation near;*
> *His presence makes me free indeed and he will soon appear.*
> *He wills that I should holy be: who can withstand his will?*
> *The counsel of his grace in me he surely shall fulfill.*
> *Jesus, I hang upon your Word: I steadfastly believe*
> *You will return and claim me, Lord, and to yourself receive.*

Leader's Notes

Leading a Bible discussion can be an enjoyable and rewarding experience. But it can also be *scary*—especially if you've never done it before. If this is your feeling, you're in good company. When God asked Moses to lead the Israelites out of Egypt, he replied, "O Lord, please send someone else to do it!" (Ex 4:13). It was the same with Solomon, Jeremiah and Timothy, but God helped these people in spite of their weaknesses, and he will help you as well.

You don't need to be an expert on the Bible or a trained teacher to lead a Bible discussion. The idea behind these inductive studies is that the leader guides group members to discover for themselves what the Bible has to say. This method of learning will allow group members to remember much more of what is said than a lecture would.

These studies are designed to be led easily. As a matter of fact, the flow of questions through the passage from observation to interpretation to application is so natural that you may feel that the studies lead themselves. This study guide is also flexible. You can use it with a variety of groups—student, professional, neighborhood or church groups. Each study takes forty-five to sixty minutes in a group setting.

There are some important facts to know about group dynamics and encouraging discussion. The suggestions listed below should enable you to effectively and enjoyably fulfill your role as leader.

Preparing for the Study

1. Ask God to help you understand and apply the passage in your own life. Unless this happens, you will not be prepared to lead others. Pray too for the various members of the group. Ask God to open your hearts to the message of his Word and motivate you to action.

2. Read the introduction to the entire guide to get an overview of the entire book and the issues which will be explored.

3. As you begin each study, read and reread the assigned Bible passage to familiarize yourself with it.

4. This study guide is based on the New International Version of the Bible. It will help you and the group if you use this translation as the basis for your study and discussion.

5. Carefully work through each question in the study. Spend time in meditation and reflection as you consider how to respond.

6. Write your thoughts and responses in the space provided in the study guide. This will help you to express your understanding of the passage clearly.

7. It might help to have a Bible dictionary handy. Use it to look up any unfamiliar words, names or places. (For additional help on how to study a passage, see chapter five of *How to Lead a LifeGuide Bible Study,* InterVarsity Press.)

8. Consider how you can apply the Scripture to your life. Remember that the group will follow your lead in responding to the studies. They will not go any deeper than you do.

9. Once you have finished your own study of the passage, familiarize yourself with the leader's notes for the study you are leading. These are designed to help you in several ways. First, they tell you the purpose the study guide author had in mind when writing the study. Take time to think through how the study questions work together to accomplish that purpose. Second, the notes provide you with additional background information or suggestions on group dynamics for various questions. This information can be useful when people have difficulty understanding or answering a question. Third, the leader's notes can alert you to potential problems you may encounter during the study.

10. If you wish to remind yourself of anything mentioned in the leader's notes, make a note to yourself below that question in the study.

Leading the Study

1. Begin the study on time. Open with prayer, asking God to help the group to understand and apply the passage.

2. Be sure that everyone in your group has a study guide. Encourage the group to prepare beforehand for each discussion by reading the introduction to the guide and by working through the questions in the study.

3. At the beginning of your first time together, explain that these studies are meant to be discussions, not lectures. Encourage the members of the group to participate. However, do not put pressure on those who may be hesitant to speak during the first few sessions. You may want to suggest the following guidelines to your group.

☐ Stick to the topic being discussed.

☐ Your responses should be based on the verses which are the focus of the discussion and not on outside authorities such as commentaries or speakers.

☐ These studies focus on a particular passage of Scripture. Only rarely should you refer to other portions of the Bible. This allows for everyone to participate in in-depth study on equal ground.

☐ Anything said in the group is considered confidential and will not be discussed outside the group unless specific permission is given to do so.

☐ We will listen attentively to each other and provide time for each person present to talk.

☐ We will pray for each other.

4. Have a group member read the introduction at the beginning of the discussion.

5. Every session begins with a group discussion question. The question or activity is meant to be used before the passage is read. The question introduces the theme of the study and encourages group members to begin to open up. Encourage as many members as possible to participate, and be ready to get the discussion going with your own response.

This section is designed to reveal where our thoughts or feelings need to be transformed by Scripture. That is why it is especially important not to read the passage before the discussion question is asked. The passage will tend to color the honest reactions people would otherwise give because they are, of course, supposed to think the way the Bible does.

You may want to supplement the group discussion question with an icebreaker to help people to get comfortable. See the community section of *Small Group Idea Book* for more ideas.

You also might want to use the personal reflection question with your group. Either allow a time of silence for people to respond individually or discuss it together.

6. Have a group member (or members if the passage is long) read aloud the passage to be studied. Then give people several minutes to read the passage again silently so that they can take it all in.

7. Question 1 will generally be an overview question designed to briefly survey the passage. Encourage the group to look at the whole passage, but try to avoid getting sidetracked by questions or issues that will be addressed later in the study.

8. As you ask the questions, keep in mind that they are designed to be used just as they are written. You may simply read them aloud. Or you may prefer to express them in your own words.

There may be times when it is appropriate to deviate from the study guide. For example, a question may have already been answered. If so, move on to the next question. Or someone may raise an important question not covered in the guide. Take time to discuss it, but try to keep the group from going off on tangents.

9. Avoid answering your own questions. If necessary, repeat or rephrase them until they are clearly understood. Or point out something you read in the leader's notes to clarify the context or meaning. An eager group quickly becomes passive and silent if they think the leader will do most of the talking.

10. Don't be afraid of silence. People may need time to think about the question before formulating their answers.

11. Don't be content with just one answer. Ask, "What do the rest of you think?" or "Anything else?" until several people have given answers to the question.

12. Acknowledge all contributions. Try to be affirming whenever possible. Never reject an answer. If it is clearly off-base, ask, "Which verse led you to that conclusion?" or again, "What do the rest of you think?"

13. Don't expect every answer to be addressed to you, even though this will probably happen at first. As group members become more at ease, they will begin to truly interact with each other. This is one sign of healthy discussion.

14. Don't be afraid of controversy. It can be very stimulating. If you don't resolve an issue completely, don't be frustrated. Move on and keep it in mind for later. A subsequent study may solve the problem.

15. Periodically summarize what the group has said about the passage. This helps to draw together the various ideas mentioned and gives continuity to the study. But don't preach.

16. At the end of the Bible discussion you may want to allow group members a time of quiet to work on an idea under "Now or Later." Then discuss what you experienced. Or you may want to encourage group members to work on these ideas between meetings. Give an opportunity during the session for people to talk about what they are learning.

17. Conclude your time together with conversational prayer, adapting the prayer suggestion at the end of the study to your group. Ask for God's help in following through on the commitments you've made.

18. End on time.

Many more suggestions and helps are found in *How to Lead a LifeGuide Bible Study*.

Components of Small Groups

A healthy small group should do more than study the Bible. There are four components to consider as you structure your time together.

Nurture. Small groups help us to grow in our knowledge and love of God. Bible study is the key to making this happen and is the foundation of your small group.

Community. Small groups are a great place to develop deep friendships with other Christians. Allow time for informal interaction before and after each study. Plan activities and games that will help you get to know each other. Spend time having fun together going on a picnic or cooking dinner together.

Worship and prayer. Your study will be enhanced by spending time praising God together in prayer or song. Pray for each other's needs and keep
track of how God is answering prayer in your group. Ask God to help you to
apply what you are learning in your study.

Outreach. Reaching out to others can be a practical way of applying what
you are learning, and it will keep your group from becoming self-focused.
Host a series of evangelistic discussions for your friends or neighbors. Clean
up the yard of an elderly friend. Serve at a soup kitchen together, or spend a
day working on a Habitat house.

Many more suggestions and helps in each of these areas are found in
Small Group Idea Book. Information on building a small group can be found
in *Small Group Leaders' Handbook* and *The Big Book on Small Groups* (both
from InterVarsity Press). Reading through one of these books would be
worth your time.

Study 1. What Is My Time Worth? Ecclesiastes 3:1-14; 12:1-14.

Purpose: To see time as a gift from God and then examine our use of time for
its current and eternal worth.

Question 2. The poet tells us (rightly) that God "has made everything beautiful in its time." Even though some of the twenty-eight kinds of time mentioned in the poem seem negative, we are challenged to catch a glimpse of
God's view even in hardship. You will return to this area later in the study,
so make a mental or written note of which word best describes the current
season of your life.

Question 3. Nearly every phrase of the author's commentary on this poem
connects or contrasts divine and human perspective. In order to capture any
sense of the value of time we must recognize both. For humans, note that
workers can reasonably look for gain; that we have some sense of eternity
but can't fully understand it; that we can seek happiness, do good and find
satisfaction in our work; that we are to revere God. God, on the other hand,
is in charge of both time and eternity. He is the one who lays a burden on
mortals, but he has also made everything beautiful in its time; he has given
us the concept of eternity and also the tension of not fully understanding
it; he gives us gifts of time, eternity, labor and satisfaction. Only what God
does will last forever, and we cannot by our own design add or subtract from
that.

Question 4. Examining the text with question three is bound to lead to
a measure of frustration. Upon reflection it can also lead to hope, and we
would do well to identify both. Michael Eaton, a pastor and professor in
Johannesburg, wrote in the Tyndale Old Testament Commentary on Ecclesiastes, "The thrust of the passage is that man is offered a life that is joyful

but not self-sufficient" (*Ecclesiastes* [Downers Grove, Ill.: InterVarsity Press, 1983], p. 80). He continues, "Our consciousness of God is part of our nature, and the suppression of it is part of our sin" (p. 81). Even our frustration over time when it comes to the divine-human difference may itself be a gift from God, a magnet drawing us to himself. The early theologian Augustine of Hippo (A.D. 354-430) opens his *Confessions* with his famous dictum, "You have made us for yourself and our hearts find no peace until they rest in you" (1.1).

Question 5. Thursday's plans may be quite ordinary, as ordinary as eating and drinking and going to work. One of God's gifts is to find satisfaction, even in ordinary time. Begin to anticipate that for your next Thursday—and plan accordingly.

Question 7. Overall this poem depicts a purposeless old man nearing the end of his time on earth. Look through the metaphors for aging in these verses. You will find playful pictures of eyes, ears, teeth, sleeplessness, hair, arms, legs, even sex.

Question 9. If you have trouble with the original question, ask the more simple, "Do you agree or disagree? Why?" Even though the writer of Ecclesiastes complains constantly that everything is meaningless, he has shown throughout his book a higher value than is visible to the human eye. Much of this value rests in time—when seen from God's perspective. His own opening and this closing chapter help us respond to his very human complaint.

Question 10. Revisit the overused Joseph of this study's introduction. Consider God's value on how Joseph might spend his evening, as well as the disabilities of the elderly neighbor which will eventually be visited also on Joseph. Notice what Ecclesiastes 12:1 might mean in Joseph's setting—and how he might observe that bit of wise instruction. Consider whether fixing his neighbor's computer would come under God's description of "beautiful." Is there some way that Joseph can find God's gift of enjoyment in that work? Or might his time be better spent doing . . . ?

Study 2. Use or Lose? Matthew 25:14-30.

Purpose: To value the skills, opportunities and assets that God has entrusted to us and to use them wisely for his purposes.

Question 2. Work only with verses 14-23 for this question. The third servant had a different experience with the master, partly because he did not recognize the master's true nature. The text shows that the master was generous, that he knew each servant's ability and gave accordingly, that he had property and trusted his servants to care for that property in his absence, that he was gone a long time and therefore could afford a lengthy trip, that he encouraged these servants by calling them "good and faithful," that he increased their responsibility based on how they had served in his absence, that he invited them to "share" in his "happiness" (which assumes that he wanted them to succeed), and that he was willing to share not only goods but enjoyment with them. They and their work were valuable to him. He delighted in their success.

Question 4. Notice the importance of the words *entrusted* and *ability*. This parable assumes differing abilities and differing opportunities. Life is not a level playing field. The master acknowledged those differences and gave differing levels of responsibility accordingly. We can assume that the third servant could have managed the one talent just fine—had he chosen to do so.

Question 5. In Matthew's era a "talent" was a large unit of money. Later the English language adopted the term from this parable to refer to some inborn ability or skill, thus capturing the concept that a "talent" is endowed or given, and that the results are greater than what could be achieved by hard work alone.

Christians believe that all that we are and all that we have comes from God. As we work with this question about what God has "entrusted" to us, we can consider time, opportunities, money, education, possessions, heritage, relationships, people and position, as well as skills or physical prowess. If God has "entrusted" us with this, he will rightly expect an accounting so that we too can "share [our] master's happiness." Try focusing on one particular "talent" that God has "entrusted" to you as you continue your work with this text.

Question 6. Only at this point do we begin to look at the third servant. By now we know the character of the master through his relationship with the first two servants. This section of the text tells more about the character of the third servant than it reveals of his master. We can guess what this servant planned to do with his master's one talent if by chance the master did not return at all. Only the servant would know its hiding place. Since this parable immediately follows Jesus' teaching about the end of time and his return, the third servant represents all of us who handle what God has entrusted to us as if there is no return with its subsequent accounting.

Question 7. This servant failed to understand that his master would come back, that the master expected his servants to use what was entrusted to them, that he knew the hidden motives of his servant and that the consequence of non-use would be serious—for him.

Question 8. The master entrusted his money to each of the three servants "according to his ability" (v. 15). It was the third servant alone who did not trust his master, nor did he even recognize his master's true benevolent nature—a caution to us when our faith lags.

Question 9. All of the servants had a responsibility to carry out a "worthy" use of whatever the master entrusted to them. The third servant proved himself "worthless." As a follow-up question consider: What might the other two servants learn from witnessing this final scene of the story?

Study 3. Why Work? 2 Thessalonians 3:6-15.
Purpose: To adopt God's value of work and to help others achieve the benefits of work to the extent that they are able.
Question 2. Groups may want to divide up and have individuals or groups of two or three each look up one of the passages and report back to the group.
From these four combined texts, create a list of reasons to work. *From 2 Thessalonians 3:* Paul worked at manual labor as an example to others as Zane might become an example to his own child. Work allows us to not be a burden to others. It provides food which must otherwise be earned by someone else. Not working creates shame, lack of self-respect. *From 1 Thessalonians 4:* Work earns respect from nonbelievers and therefore reflects on Christ himself. *From Ephesians 4:* Work reduces the temptation to steal. It provides enough excess that we can and should share with people in need. *From 1 Timothy 5:* Work is part of the God-given responsibility to care for our families, as important as faith itself.
Questions 4-5. "Work," of course, does not just mean paid employment. Even if you do not currently have a job, you are still in roles (such as parent, child, sibling, friend, church member) that require work. You also still have general daily responsibilities that come with being an adult.
Question 7. Paul condemns idleness but not leisure, though leisure was probably viewed with less entitlement in that era than in Western culture today. Zane seems to have merged them in his thinking. How can you have a spiritually healthy distinction?
Question 8. Conroy might find it easier to create a long-range plan than to deal with Zane's current crisis. Or he might find writing a check easier than going with Zane to the store and showing him how to resolve his most urgent needs as economically as possible. Explore options for Conroy that are genuinely helpful in the short term without creating dependency or unwarranted expectations. In addition, Conroy's responsibility as "Christian brother" might include spiritual admonition as well as guidance in helping Zane change his whole approach to work.
Now or Later. These texts suggest a number of options for Conroy. He can be the same kind of model for Zane that Paul was for the church of Thessalonica. Paul worked during his visit there; he was not a burden for others. Conroy can urge Zane to "settle down and earn the bread" that he and his family need (2 Thess 3:12)—though it seems that hunger is already upon him and, more significantly, on his family.

These passages also suggest the option of isolating Zane, refusing to have anything to do with him so that he "may feel ashamed" (2 Thess 3:14). Yet Zane already expresses a sense of shame in the manner of his request. And Zane's family is in more danger than he is.

You may come up with other options. Consider the implications for each person involved, as well as the implications for "onlookers," as you create a plan.

Study 4. Trustworthy? Luke 16:1-15.

Purpose: To begin to make financial decisions with an eye toward eternal purpose.

Question 1. Notice words and actions so that you can give some evaluation of the moral qualities of the major characters: the rich man, the manager and the various debtors.

Questions 3-5. Notice why the manager was losing his job (v. 1) and also his motives for reducing the bills (v. 4). However, also note that Bible scholars differ on how this parable might best be interpreted. Some say that the shrewd and soon-to-be-unemployed manager was giving away his commission and thus gaining gratitude toward himself from his former master's current customers. Others note that verse 8 speaks of the manager as "dishonest" which suggests that it was his master's money, not his own, that was at stake here. The owner is therefore commending his shrewdness (but obviously not his honesty).

The key to the parable is probably the rather confusing verse 9. Here we must assume that Jesus is *not* suggesting that his disciples try to buy their way into heaven. This would conflict with teachings throughout the New Testament that salvation is by grace through faith—not bought by either money or deeds. What is more likely is that Jesus is instructing his followers to invest their money in people and causes that have eternal consequences. The manager serves as an example of this in that he's planning ahead and making choices with the future in mind. Our money and material possessions are only for our time on earth and won't come with us or matter once we die, Jesus reminds us, so we need to use them in ways that have eternal value.

Giving generously and helping meet the needs of others wins us friends here on earth and has eternal consequences in that it helps establish and spread Jesus' kingdom. It also pleases our Father. Consider ways you might use your energies and funds in a heaven-focused way, in ways that will glorify Christ and point others toward him.

Question 6. When Jesus comments on the parable (vv. 9-13), he comes back to the manager's motive—but with an adjustment that suggests a larger view of God and a less self-focused motive. (Compare v. 4 with v. 9.) R. T. France comments in the *New Bible Commentary,* "If we mistakenly view God as a hard taskmaster, it will be hard for us to respond to him in a loving and open way. We are to use his gifts responsibly, but also adventurously. That is the way to be ready for the *parousia* [return of Christ]" (G. J. Wenham, J. A. Motyer, D. A. Carson and R. T. France, eds., 21st Century Ed. [Downers Grove, Ill.: InterVarsity Press, 1994], p. 1006).

Questions 8-9. In the usual tensions of how to run a church, church leaders often debate whether we should use a business model or a shepherd model. In this parable Jesus seems to assume that good business is not necessarily bad discipleship. Wise leaders will be alert to what they can borrow from the best of business practice. But they should not confuse the two. We can borrow from business only when the techniques do not conflict with the higher value of an eternal perspective that brings glory to Christ, and prepares his followers for eternity with him. Suppose, for example, that the manager in this parable is a member as well as an employee of your church—and you are one of the church leaders. How might you carry out your business responsibility while simultaneously honoring the eternal principles taught in this text? Would/should we handle our workweek responsibilities any differently?

Study 5. What's Tempting About Power? Matthew 20:1-28.
Purpose: To gain awareness of the temptations of power and to resist these by using power in a Christ-honoring way.
Question 1. Power is woven throughout these three scenes. Use this question to make an extensive survey of the passage.
Question 2. Work your way through the parable again, this time visualizing several scenes. How might you try to capture one scene that you find particularly compelling?
Question 4. We may speculate about the landowner's motive. (Did he feel sorry for those who did not yet have work? Were the first workers that he hired not getting the job done as quickly as he hoped? Was it easier to hand out the same coin to everyone rather than keep a time sheet and calculate fractions of the day? Was he merely following a whim?) Was this "executive" fair or unfair? Does it matter? Verse 15 simply states the facts of power with an assumed answer: "Don't I have the *right* to do what I want with *my own* money?"

The landowner's next question looks at the motives of those who complained: envy. And the virtue of the landowner: generosity. In his mind they were asking the wrong question. Fairness was not an issue. Each worker had received as much or more than he expected. The more subtle qualities of envy and generosity show up here as by-products of power. We will need to keep "byproducts" in mind as we look at our own use and misuse of power.
Question 5. At the minimum the disciples will know to expect the unex-

pected. They can know that those with extravagant power may voluntarily take lower places. Or those with little to recommend them may be given places of honor. Our normal power rankings will have little relevance in his kingdom.

We may well wonder what Jesus meant by the term "kingdom of heaven." Scholars have come to at least three different conclusions: the kingdom of heaven (also called kingdom of God) is a new era between God and humans that Jesus ushers in with his presence on earth and his soon-to-come death and resurrection. Or, the kingdom of heaven is eternity in heaven with all whom Christ has redeemed. Or, the kingdom of heaven is Christ-followers living by Christ-taught ways among each other and toward outsiders during their time on earth. These are not necessarily mutually exclusive descriptions.

Question 6. Notice the power about to be exercised by Jesus, the priests, the teachers and the Gentiles, and the power this information might give to the disciples. Eventually we see that power itself appears morally neutral. But power is by definition a strong force. How we use the power given us can produce much good—or much harm. This would be a good spot to begin examining whether our personal use of power tends to be selfish or selfless.

Question 7. Picture each person in the scene and notice the motives that their words, actions, requests and complaints seem to suggest. We can't escape the obvious insensitivity to what Jesus has just told them in the preceding paragraph. Like many of us, their gut response was, *What's in it for me?* Even so, Jesus continues to teach them and to prepare them for all that is to come.

Question 9. "Inner housekeeping" might include examination of motives, or envisioning likely scenes ahead of time so that you anticipate the temptation to "lord it over" someone and can then plan a different response mentally, in words and in action. It is often our thoughts about other people that lead us to arrogance over them. We can name to ourselves likely candidates for this kind of mistreatment from us and begin to pray for that person and to remind ourselves of the good qualities God has given to them. When our desire becomes one of preferring their well-being over our own, we will begin to pick the path of a servant leader. Consider these and other ways you can approach this universal temptation.

Question 10. Find encouragement in other Christians who have shown you the beginnings of this difficult path. God has given some form of power to each of us. It is a gift that brings both temptation and responsibility. We can use it well, which is his intent.

Study 6. How Much Is Enough? Ecclesiastes 5:8-20.

Purpose: To find enjoyment in the gifts of work and money that God has given us, regardless of what type and amount.

Question 1. Use this question to survey the whole passage, noting three different points of view. One simple set of titles you could use is "group-focused," "self-focused," "God-focused." Other forms of titles will serve just as well. Creativity is a bonus.

Question 3. Notice particularly Matthew 20:25-28 and your reflections on question eight of study five.

Question 5. Be as specific as possible as you think through your probable reaction. (You may be doing some of it already!) Notice also the life descriptions in the text: "meaningless" (v. 10) and "grievous evil" (vv. 13, 16). Derek Kidner, writing in *The Message of Ecclesiastes*, observes: "If anything is worse than the addiction money brings, it is the emptiness it leaves. Man, with eternity in his heart, needs better nourishment than this." He goes on to say, "At this point we have to be reminded that such a man may be asking of life more than it can give. If his plans were made just on the strength of what lay within reach and what promised some security, he was looking in the wrong direction" ([Downers Grove, Ill.: InterVarsity Press, 1976], pp. 56, 58).

Question 6. God is mentioned four times in this short paragraph. Even though work and money remain the subject, the perspective shifts. Instead of "meaningless" and "grievous evil" we find words like "satisfaction," "enjoy," "gladness." Consider how our life-perspective changes if we are able to see the ordinary exchange of work and money as a gift from God.

Question 9. God's measure of success and the good life is not weighed in hours and dollars. Even in this text we see a small measure of complacency: "accept his lot" (v. 19). This is not an excuse for laziness or sloppy planning, but it is an invitation to see both work and wealth (small or great) as gifts from God. Though forward planning is important, God invites us to enjoy the now as his gift to us. So we do not work and save so that finally we can enjoy. We work and save and enjoy the process. This might lead us to change jobs in order to earn and save more money. But we might unwrap the same gift by finding ways to enjoy our present income and our present work—each day.

Question 10. Spend some moments picturing this man: his manner, his humor, his stories, his values, how he spends his day. (You may be looking at your future self.) Kidner writes: "We catch a glimpse of the man for whom life passes swiftly, not because it is short and meaningless but because, by the grace of God, he finds it utterly absorbing" (*Message of Ecclesiastes*, pp. 58-59).

Study 7. Does My Property Own Me? Luke 12:13-34.

Purpose: To hold tightly to Jesus but loosely to our possessions.

Question 2. The farmer in this story seems to be taking responsible care of the crops God has given him. Yet Jesus uses him as an example of foolishness. This is worrisome to any of us who use a cupboard, closet, garage or barn. Yet it is not the barn-building itself Jesus criticizes, but the farmer's assumption about its long-term value. Leon Morris writes, "A man whose life hangs by a thread and who may be called upon at any time to give account of himself is a fool if he relies on material things" (*The Gospel According to St. Luke,* Tyndale New Testament Commentaries [Grand Rapids: Eerdmans, 1974], p. 233).

Question 3. Work with the important phrase "rich toward God." What does it mean? How might the farmer get there? How might you?

Question 5. This text includes at least nine commands: Watch out! Be on your guard against greed (v. 15); do not worry (vv. 22, 29); consider the ravens and lilies (vv. 24, 27); do not set your heart on food (v. 29); seek God's kingdom (v. 31); do not be afraid but focus on the kingdom of God (v. 32); sell your possessions (v. 33); give to the poor (v. 33); provide purses for yourself filled with treasure in heaven (v. 33). Select one of these commands that might represent an appropriate way in your current setting for you to set your heart on God's kingdom. (Note: God does not usually ask us to neglect the responsibilities of ordinary life and people in our care.)

Question 6. Much of our heart-work is inner. It's not what we do but why. Some of this can begin with a more self-disciplined way of thinking about people and things and our own responsibility for both. A heart turned toward Christ will always have eternity in view. This need not detract from the ability to enjoy the gifts God gives us; instead, it recognizes their divine source and their temporary nature. We can also begin to cultivate a generosity of thought toward those who have less than we do, since generosity is the opposite of greed. If we allow our minds to jump not to blame but rather to opportunity with and for them, we can begin to hold our own possessions more lightly. We are thus freed to enjoy them—or to give them away, whichever seems in the best long-range interest for all involved. In addition, we can begin to explore or expand our spiritual disciplines such as prayer, Scripture reading, fasting (from use of certain things), worship, solitude, service. Practicing these will help turn our heart toward more eternal values—and to God himself.

Question 9. Notice the characteristics of God revealed in verses 32-34, then back up and look at his kindly care throughout the text. This passage holds much in common with the parable of the talents studied in study two. Both invite us to focus on the character of God.

Study 8. How Much Is Too Much? 1 Timothy 6:3-10, 17-20.

Purpose: To find contentment in the godly use of whatever money God allows us.

Question 1. Use this question to survey the entire text, highlighting particularly any allusion to money. Notice that many of the concepts here do not relate precisely to money, but to the needs and responsibilities and attitudes that accompany our financial status.

Question 3. If you are in a group, consider asking one or two people to work with each of the four texts and then report to the whole group. In addition to the four texts listed from the words of Jesus, note also that Paul alludes to Job 1:12 and Ecclesiastes 5:15 (Paul studied these books too!).

Question 4. Paul may have had any number of reasons for giving this warning. Were religious leaders in Ephesus charging money in exchange for some secret truths available only to them? These Gnostic types of belief are not as frequently embedded in today's Christianity as they seem to have been in Timothy's time and place. We do, however, see variations of the "prosperity gospel," which might be expressed as, "If I am good to God, he will be good to me." Or "If I give my money to this cause or person, God will give it back to me tenfold—and maybe more." Or "God wants to make all of his people prosperous, and it's only our own shortcomings that keep him from giving us all that we want." Yet Paul's coaching of Timothy regarding money does not point that direction at all. Indeed it points the opposite direction. Contentment is of more value than money; godliness with contentment is even better. He speaks of efforts to get rich as a "temptation" and a "trap." He echoes Jesus' statements on the danger of loving money and even sees the love of money as a threat to faith.

One of the many shortcomings in today's versions of the prosperity gospel is that it assumes that God owes us prosperity in exchange for our good behavior. Yet the whole of Scripture speaks of God as sovereign and owing nothing to anyone—ever. He gives out of grace and generosity and asks us to do the same. If Christians think of prosperity as their just earnings from God, they can lose track of their own sinfulness. In contrast, godly Christians who continue to endure suffering and never become wealthy can sink into self-blame, unable to see God's kindness and love even in the midst of suffering. Further, their more wealthy brothers and sisters aren't likely to enter into their suffering with shared help and comfort because, in the back of their minds, they may see the poor as getting what they deserve. In essence the prosperity gospel denies God's gifts and turns them into perceived earnings for good behavior. It reduces our ability to trust God even through pain and loss, and provides little incentive to find contentment in whatever God gives us—whether wealth or poverty. In the end, this view of God's rewards ends with prosperity in this life, not an easy preparation for eternity with him.

Question 5. Consider role-playing a conversation with Madabuku. Work at being sensitive to his religious culture. Ask about his desires, motives, hopes and subsequent theological perspective. Keep coming back to Jesus—his example and his teachings.

Question 7. Notice that the word *gain* in verse 6 has a far broader and a far more lasting meaning than the financial gain of verse 5. Visualize this person and mentally get to know him or her. Can you see yourself in that picture, maybe at some future date?

Question 8. Like most pastors today, Timothy may have found it a bit daunting to "command" anything to the rich in his church. But notice the common good of the church that is possible through the generosity of those who are rich. And if the ultimate goal of money is not a certain degree of wealth but instead the emotional and spiritual gain of contentment, then these are precisely the kinds of actions that will provide "life that is truly life" (v. 19). A follow-up question might be: What attitudes about money do these commands reflect?

Question 10. Paul ends his instructions to Timothy by saying that he and the people of his church should "take hold of the life that is truly life." His instructions about the tensions between money and "godliness with contentment" (v. 6) hold value for all of us: those who need more money than they have, those who have a surplus of money and even those who live by subsistence. Questions of self examination might include: Does my desire for or protection of my money keep me from finding contentment? Am I able to find contentment with no financial outlay at all and, if so, how and where? Am I generous or protective with my money? Does my money or my search for money take away from my godliness? How do I feel about people who are richer (or poorer) than I am? Am I able to feel their need or enjoy their enjoyment? Am I able to use my own money in unselfish and un-self-conscious ways?

The title question of this study is, How much is too much? No dollar amount will fully answer that question. But the answers come from examining how well we are able to practice "godliness with contentment" and how or if we allow our financial situation to detract from what Paul describes as this less measurable "great gain."

Study 9. Why Give? 1 Chronicles 29:1-20.
Purpose: To recognize God as the source of our assets (both tangible and intangible) and to then give joyfully out of praise and thanks to God.

Question 1. Enjoy this complex scene as you garner information from throughout the text. Note: The coin "daric" referred to in verse 7 came into use during the reign of King Darius of Persia (521-486 B.C.), which may show when the records of the Chronicles were compiled. Also, the term *talent* is used throughout Scripture with a variety of understandings in meaning. It might mean two sacks of gold or of silver. "Talent" might also be a literary way of saying "lots and lots of money" (I. Howard Marshall, A. R. Millard,

J. I. Packer and D. J. Wiseman, eds., *New Bible Dictionary*, 3rd ed. [Downers Grove, Ill.: InterVarsity Press, 1996], p. 790).

Question 3. Gifts now and in David's era come in many forms in addition to money. Consider time, skills, opportunities and relationships as well as material objects. Notice the organizational steps in this huge gathering, the example of leaders, the atmosphere of generosity, the corporate rejoicing and devotion to God. The people and the leaders rejoice together. Even the skills of the craftsmen were consecrated to God. Might we equally rejoice over the skills of our church janitor or Web designer, and commission people as kingdom-builders in their homes and workplaces?

Question 6. If you're working with a group, consider insisting on prayers of only one or two sentences at a time. This will allow people who are uncomfortable praying aloud to contribute briefly in a non-threatening way. Also, invite your group to feel comfortable during moments of silence between prayers and to use that time to mentally echo each other's words and make them their own.

If you're using this study alone, take as long as you want on this prayer exercise. Make notes of what you might want to continue in the "Now or Later" section at the close of the study.

Question 7. David's practice of giving (and encouraging his people to do the same) grows out of his view of how God and his people relate to one another. You'll find evidence of this in almost every phrase of this portion of his prayer. Explore their compiled meaning.

Question 9. Take particular note of the intimacy and urgency in words such as *willing, consecrate, self, today.*

Question 10. If you're in a group, consider compiling together suggestions about how to pray for Jason by following David's pattern and concept of God. Or draft written prayers and share them with one another. If you're studying alone and you happen to know a "Jason," pray David's prayer with your own elaborations, using that child's name.

Study 10. What If I Lose It All? Job 1:1-22; 19:17-27.

Purpose: To contemplate the possibility of major loss, but to also fortify ourselves by borrowing Job's hope and faith.

Question 5. Once the wager has been set, God, Job and even Satan are all on trial. Satan has charged that Job believes God only because God protects him from harm and even gives him wonderful gifts by blessing his work. In his present circumstances of prosperity Job's faith is constantly rewarded. So for the sake of his own honor God permits the series of tragic losses which puts Job on trial, even though Job does not know the cause. The test will show whether Job's faith is a mere game of "give and get" or whether his faith is in God himself, not just what he can gain from God. God, on the other hand, is also on trial. Does he attract followers only by enticing them with treats? Or is God true and right and holy and worthy of worship quite apart from his gifts? Even Satan is on trial. What if this commitment of God to his people and them to him holds firm beyond an expected system of benefits? What if that connection is rooted in love? What if it is eternal? What if the system is not commercial, but covenantal?

Question 7. Huge loss can trigger huge temptation. Though Job could not witness the scene recorded in the first part of the chapter, he knew God's character—and trusted in that, even though he had no explanation for God's acts. He acknowledged that the gifts of family and belongings came from God but also accepted that the removal of these gifts did not happen apart from God's permission. To think otherwise would assume a God who is less than almighty. Even so, "Job did not sin by charging God with wrongdoing."

Question 9. Readers can hardly find a more succinct statement of Judeo-Christian faith than Job's mere sentence beginning, "I know that my Redeemer lives." Even the Apostles' Creed borrows from it with its phrase, "I believe in . . . the resurrection of the body." In answer to this question you will find that (1) Job understands the significance and importance of his words and thus believes they ought to be recorded forever; (2) he personally will see God; (3) *in his own flesh* (already decaying with boils) he will see God—a hint of what the apostle Paul will call the resurrected body, an "imperishable" body, a "spiritual body," in 1 Corinthians 15; and (4) his Redeemer is the eternal world conqueror—God himself.

Paul Stevens writes in his *Job: Wrestling with God* LifeGuide Bible study: "The idea of a redeemer comes from the Hebrew understanding of the solidarity of the family. The redeemer or kinsman is a brother, father, or cousin who is involved in everything one does, sharing guilt or avenging an enemy. . . . That God himself should become Job's nearest relative and vindicate him forever—on whichever side of the grave he might be—is surely the highest point of revelation in this book, and can be rightly called 'The Gospel According to Job.' It will take the New Testament to fully develop what that Redeemer must do . . . making us a son or daughter in God's family" ([Downers Grove, Ill.: InterVarsity Press, 2003], p. 81).

Carolyn Nystrom is a freelance writer based in the western Chicago suburbs. She has written more than eighty books and Bible study guides, including Never Beyond Hope *and* Praying *(both with J. I. Packer) and* Clouds of Witnesses *(with Mark Noll). Her other LifeGuide Bible studies include* 1 & 2 Peter and Jude, Integrity *and* Old Testament Characters. *She also served as general editor for the Christian Classics series.*